A treatise on the universal spread of the Gospel, the glorious millenium, and the second coming of Christ. By Joseph Sutcliffe.

Joseph Sutcliffe

A treatise on the universal spread of the Gospel, the glorious millenium, and the second coming of Christ. By Joseph Sutcliffe.
Sutcliffe, Joseph
ESTCID: T180683
Reproduction from John Rylands University Library of Manchester

Doncaster : printed at the Gazette-Office by W. Sheardown, 1798.
24p. ; 12°

Eighteenth Century
Collections Online
Print Editions

Gale ECCO Print Editions

Relive history with *Eighteenth Century Collections Online*, now available in print for the independent historian and collector. This series includes the most significant English-language and foreign-language works printed in Great Britain during the eighteenth century, and is organized in seven different subject areas including literature and language; medicine, science, and technology; and religion and philosophy. The collection also includes thousands of important works from the Americas.

The eighteenth century has been called "The Age of Enlightenment." It was a period of rapid advance in print culture and publishing, in world exploration, and in the rapid growth of science and technology – all of which had a profound impact on the political and cultural landscape. At the end of the century the American Revolution, French Revolution and Industrial Revolution, perhaps three of the most significant events in modern history, set in motion developments that eventually dominated world political, economic, and social life.

In a groundbreaking effort, Gale initiated a revolution of its own: digitization of epic proportions to preserve these invaluable works in the largest online archive of its kind. Contributions from major world libraries constitute over 175,000 original printed works. Scanned images of the actual pages, rather than transcriptions, recreate the works *as they first appeared.*

Now for the first time, these high-quality digital scans of original works are available via print-on-demand, making them readily accessible to libraries, students, independent scholars, and readers of all ages.

For our initial release we have created seven robust collections to form one the world's most comprehensive catalogs of 18th century works.

Initial Gale ECCO Print Editions collections include:

History and Geography
Rich in titles on English life and social history, this collection spans the world as it was known to eighteenth-century historians and explorers. Titles include a wealth of travel accounts and diaries, histories of nations from throughout the world, and maps and charts of a world that was still being discovered. Students of the War of American Independence will find fascinating accounts from the British side of conflict.

Social Science

Delve into what it was like to live during the eighteenth century by reading the first-hand accounts of everyday people, including city dwellers and farmers, businessmen and bankers, artisans and merchants, artists and their patrons, politicians and their constituents. Original texts make the American, French, and Industrial revolutions vividly contemporary.

Medicine, Science and Technology

Medical theory and practice of the 1700s developed rapidly, as is evidenced by the extensive collection, which includes descriptions of diseases, their conditions, and treatments. Books on science and technology, agriculture, military technology, natural philosophy, even cookbooks, are all contained here.

Literature and Language

Western literary study flows out of eighteenth-century works by Alexander Pope, Daniel Defoe, Henry Fielding, Frances Burney, Denis Diderot, Johann Gottfried Herder, Johann Wolfgang von Goethe, and others. Experience the birth of the modern novel, or compare the development of language using dictionaries and grammar discourses.

Religion and Philosophy

The Age of Enlightenment profoundly enriched religious and philosophical understanding and continues to influence present-day thinking. Works collected here include masterpieces by David Hume, Immanuel Kant, and Jean-Jacques Rousseau, as well as religious sermons and moral debates on the issues of the day, such as the slave trade. The Age of Reason saw conflict between Protestantism and Catholicism transformed into one between faith and logic -- a debate that continues in the twenty-first century.

Law and Reference

This collection reveals the history of English common law and Empire law in a vastly changing world of British expansion. Dominating the legal field is the *Commentaries of the Law of England* by Sir William Blackstone, which first appeared in 1765. Reference works such as almanacs and catalogues continue to educate us by revealing the day-to-day workings of society.

Fine Arts

The eighteenth-century fascination with Greek and Roman antiquity followed the systematic excavation of the ruins at Pompeii and Herculaneum in southern Italy; and after 1750 a neoclassical style dominated all artistic fields. The titles here trace developments in mostly English-language works on painting, sculpture, architecture, music, theater, and other disciplines. Instructional works on musical instruments, catalogs of art objects, comic operas, and more are also included.

The BiblioLife Network

This project was made possible in part by the BiblioLife Network (BLN), a project aimed at addressing some of the huge challenges facing book preservationists around the world. The BLN includes libraries, library networks, archives, subject matter experts, online communities and library service providers. We believe every book ever published should be available as a high-quality print reproduction; printed on-demand anywhere in the world. This insures the ongoing accessibility of the content and helps generate sustainable revenue for the libraries and organizations that work to preserve these important materials.

The following book is in the "public domain" and represents an authentic reproduction of the text as printed by the original publisher. While we have attempted to accurately maintain the integrity of the original work, there are sometimes problems with the original work or the micro-film from which the books were digitized. This can result in minor errors in reproduction. Possible imperfections include missing and blurred pages, poor pictures, markings and other reproduction issues beyond our control. Because this work is culturally important, we have made it available as part of our commitment to protecting, preserving, and promoting the world's literature.

GUIDE TO FOLD-OUTS MAPS and OVERSIZED IMAGES

The book you are reading was digitized from microfilm captured over the past thirty to forty years. Years after the creation of the original microfilm, the book was converted to digital files and made available in an online database.

In an online database, page images do not need to conform to the size restrictions found in a printed book. When converting these images back into a printed bound book, the page sizes are standardized in ways that maintain the detail of the original. For large images, such as fold-out maps, the original page image is split into two or more pages

Guidelines used to determine how to split the page image follows:

• Some images are split vertically; large images require vertical and horizontal splits.
• For horizontal splits, the content is split left to right.
• For vertical splits, the content is split from top to bottom.
• For both vertical and horizontal splits, the image is processed from top left to bottom right.

A
TREATISE

ON THE

UNIVERSAL SPREAD

OF THE

GOSPEL,

THE

Glorious Millennium,

AND THE

SECOND COMING OF CHRIST.

BY JOSEPH SUTCLIFFE

Wherefore God also hath highly exalted him, and given him a name which is
above every name: that at the name of Jesus every knee should bow,
and that every tongue should confess that Jesus Christ is Lord, to the
glory of God the Father . . . . PAUL

DONCASTER
PRINTED AT THE GAZETTE-OFFICE BY W. SHEARDOWN.

1798

Is it probable that God who foretold to a year, and very clearly, the deliverance of [Israel] from their Egyptian bondage, their return from the Babylonian captivity, the building of the second temple, and the death of the Messiah, should have been silent, or not once spoken as clearly concerning his coming to destroy the destroyers, and set up his kingdom? . . . . FLETCHER.

DURING the twelve hundred and sixty years of the Anti-christian empire, or the predominancy of priestly pomp, error, and corruption in the church, real piety has been like embers concealed in the ashes, or, if at any interval it broke forth into the enlightened flame of reformation, the clergy have used the most ingenious policy, and were wanting in no efforts to exterminate the rising sect. The Albigenses of Languedoc the Waldenses of Lyons, the Vaudois of Piedmont, and the friends of Hus in Bohemia, were nearly cut off by the military force. The Lollards in England, and the Reformed of France, have also suffered the severest persecution. The revocation of the edict of Nantes, which brought the greatest calamities on the latter, was occasioned by the particular solicitations of the clergy. God's faithful witnesses have been slain in the harlot city, and their dead bodies have laid in the streets; for their enemies could not bury them their piety and writings would still speak, and cover with silence the gain-sayers of righteousness and truth.

The first instance in which the flame broke forth into permanent reformation, and glowed with ardour which increased by resistance, was, by the bold and nervous sermons and writings of Martin Luther. The work accomplished by this intrepid monk, appears the more evidently to be of God because his opposition was without any previous design of subverting the Roman hierarchy. By preaching against the shameful sale of indulgences, he intended no more than a partial reform. But the time being come, God providentially engaged him in a controversy, which terminated in the emancipation of the north of Europe from the papal yoke. When the situation of affairs became such, that a breach with the church of Rome was unavoidable, several princes favoured the re-

---

* I have treated on this delicate subject, whom with a view to support and comfort the church, under the present inundations of vice and infidelity, with the hope of better times, and to encourage the benevolent in their laudable design to send missionaries abroad.

formation, at first secretly, and then avowedly, because they were desirous of freeing themselves from the temporal and spiritual jurisdiction of his Holiness, and of relieving their subjects of annual remittances to support the luxuries of the papal court.

From the bold and animating sermons of Luther and Melancton, great numbers of pious and learned divines in Switzerland, France, and Britain, rapidly caught the flame of reform, and warmly preached and wrote against the idolatry, errors, and corruptions of the catholics. After a long and severe contest, they succeeded in removing most of the exterior rubbish from the sanctuary, and in adorning the interior, in some degree, with the graces of regeneration.

But here we have to regret, that the venerable reformers were not more united in their religious sentiments. Those of Saxony were accused by the Swifs, of compromising the controversy with catholics concerning transubstantiation, by affirming, that the real presence was still in the bread and wine. In England this diversity of opinions was much more unhappy. One party wished to model the church after the discipline and worship of the primitive christians, and on account of their purer worship, were denominated puritans, and latterly dissenters. Another party wished to retain the pomp of robes, titles, and mitres, and what, in that dark and unsettled age, were deemed the decent splendour of the catholic devotion, and to suppress only, the supremacy of the Pope, with other absurd and idolatrous parts of the mass. The latter gained the ascendency and constitute the present national church. We lament that she did not carry her reform a little further, as it would have promoted a greater harmony of religious sentiments in this country, and given the free-thinkers of that age less occasion to reproach christianity.

In treating of the revival of piety, and of the universal spread of the gospel, it would be incompatible with christian charity to omit the work of God among the catholics. For several centuries past, a considerable number of deeply pious persons, many of whom were persons of distinction, have attempted, in their way to revive vital christianity, and have suffered much persecution on account of their pious endeavours. This great though too secret work, has been carried on chiefly by the circulation of spiritual books, and in general it may be remarked, that the writings alluded to, have peculiar excellence in treating on communion with God, and exposing the insufficiency of worldly happiness, although they have generally been deemed extremely defective in the doctrine of justification

About the year 1530, Ignatius Loyola, a Spanish nobleman, quitted the profession of arms, that he might devote himself to the conversion of the Mahometans and Heathens in every part of the earth. The benevolent heart of this man was expanded with love to all mankind, and roused to jealousy for the honour of God, by seeing the mariners hazard so much in the Indian seas for the acquisition of wealth, and nothing done by the christians for the conversion of the heathens. With a view to acquire assistance in this great work, he came to the university of Paris, and after a while, several priests were converted by his labours, and acquiesced in his design. These were constituted into a society, and entitled, 'the company of Jesus;" that is, the Jesuits; and in the generality of that order, have been deemed the most infamous of men. If it be equitable to avow my opinion, let the founders of this institution were persons of the deepest piety. The industry and perseverance, their sufferings and patience, the zeal and success of their respective missions were nearly equal to all that history has recorded of their time.

The celebrated Francis Xavier, was among the earliest converts of Ignatius. This truly apostolic man, disregarding the dignity of his birth, and forsaking his friends, made himself poor for the kingdom of God, and entered on his mission to India with invincible patience and zeal. From the year 1541 to 1552, he acquired a prodigy of languages, and with very few assistants taught and baptized incredible numbers of heathens. His mission extended from Goa to Japan, and he preached the gospel in more than fifty islands and kingdoms. His heart was chiefly fixed upon the populous empire of China, but like Moses, he was only permitted to see the land; he died, forsaken of all, in a hut upon an island near Canton, where he was going to preach. In South America, we are told, that these Jesuits taught and baptized three hundred thousand persons, and though it be admitted, that these converts were still more than semi-pagans, and that the Lord had little effect in promoting their conversion, yet considering the hatred they had to the Spaniards, and consequently to their religion, the work must have been inconceivably arduous and great. What then is not God able to do by men, who are willing to live, to lodge, or if emergency require, to labour as the poorest the then!

The numerous revivals of religion, which have taken place in every proteſtant country, during the preſent century, have been more conſiderable than any which the church has known ſince the firſt and general ſpread of the goſpel Nor has their piety been wholly confined at home. Excluſive of the emigrations of great numbers of pious people to America, and other parts, the Danes and Moravians have been extremely diligent in ſending miſſionaries abroad In England, for ſome years paſt, the minds of chriſtians have been unuſually enlarged with a deſire for the converſion of the heathen, which is a happy token, that our bleſſed Lord is about to accompliſh a glorious work in the earth. The various denominations of chriſtians, like flouriſhing branches of Chriſt the true vine, begin to vie with one another in ſending miſſionaries to the extremities of the earth On the 28th of July, 1796, twenty nine young men were ſet apart in London for the iſles in the pacific ocean, and arrived at Otaheite, after a paſſage, the moſt ſafe and ſpeedy ever known Their reception among the natives was extremely flattering Thus far God hath ſignally ſmiled upon their work In a ſermon preached on this occaſion, by Mr Burder, the converted heathens are repreſented as addreſſing the miſſionaries in theſe pathetic words, " Why did you not bring us the goſpel before ? It was known for many hundred years in your favoured iſland, thouſands, you tell us, lived and died happy in the knowledge of it, why then did you keep it from us while here ſucceſſive generations were periſhing in ſin " Vigorous and perſevering endeavours are on making to ſend a cloud of witneſſes to the Eaſt-Indies, and to China, and God will not long permit deiſtical men to obſtruct their acceſs to the Aſiatic ſhores

I am happy to find, that our principal ſeat of letters has been called upon to engage in this benevolent work Dr White, in a ſermon preached before the Univerſity of Oxford, on the duty of propagating the goſpel among our Mahometan and Gentoo ſubjects in India, illuſtrates by many ſtriking arguments, how much their condition would be ameliorated by embracing Chriſtianity. The Mahometans, in the Indoſtan empire, he obſerves, bear the proportion of one to ten " They believe in one God, Creator, and Lord of all, to whom they attribute infinite power, juſtice, and mercy. They hold the immortality of the ſoul, and expect a future judgment, a heaven and a hell, they acknowledge an univerſal providence, they honour the patriarch Abraham as the firſt author of their religion, they acknowledge Moſes and Christ to have been great prophets, and allow the gospels to be sacred books." Hence the Doctor infers, they would readily admit arguments from prophecy, and make an easy transition to Christianity —If those who derive so much wealth and authority from the church, and whose immediate duty it is to propagate the gospel, do not engage in the laudable work, God will employ others, who perhaps are more capable of communicating to the heathen, ' pure and undefiled religion."

In Europe, the revival of degenerate piety among the French, is, an object of the greatest importance towards the universal spread of the gospel. This great nation, situate in the centre of the catholic community, having abolished all persecution for religious sentiments, having annihilated the tyranical parts of the clerical power, and having exposed relics, images, and every priestly artifice, to the utmost degradation, must thereby have applained the way for the total destruction of idolatry, and afforded a favourable moment for Christianity to assume her primitive form. The literary, commercial, and colonial influence of this great nation, which might greatly contribute towards the spread of the gospel in foreign parts, must render a work of God among them, an object greatly to be desired. The accomplishment of a very remarkable prediction respecting these identical men, should awaken our expectation of some great revival among them. " And the same hour, was there a great [political] earthquake, and the tenth part of the city fell: and in the earthquake were slain of men seven thousand, and the remnant were affrighted, and gave glory to the God of heaven." It is agreed by catholic and protestant commentators on the Revelation, that France is a tenth part of the Roman beast, Rev. xiii. and of course must be a tenth part of the Papal beast, Rev. xiii. 11. And it is generally understood, that the eleventh chapter, which contains the above prediction, is, an introduction to the eleven succeeding chapters, and contains an epitome of their contents. Now, this earthquake was to take place, the same hour that the Spirit of life from God entered into the two witnesses or whole body of ministers, which is presumed to be the present period, in which France has fallen from under the power of the Pope. If the slaying of the seven thousand be referred to the million of men, which is said to have already fallen during the present war, or if we follow the Vulgate translation, Nomina Hominum, or Beza, Capita Hominum, and refer it to the suppression of titles, we must acknowledge the prophecy to have received a very ſtriking completion.

Similar to this is another diſtinguiſhed prophecy, Revelation xvi. 18, 19, which is to be accompliſhed previous to the total deſtruction of popery. " And there was a great earthquake, ſuch as was not ſince men were upon the earth, ſo mighty an earthquake, and ſo great. And the great city was divided into three parts, and the cities of the nations fell; and great Babylon came in remembrance before God, to give unto her the cup of the wine of the fierceneſs of his wrath." Our Lord ſays " A houſe divided againſt itſelf cannot ſtand;" and the Papal empire, at this period, ſtrikingly exhibits a triple diviſion,—catholics, proteſtants, and deiſts, whoſe numbers perhaps are nearly equal. Within one age after Luther, the proteſtants completely rent off a third part. Since the commencement of the preſent century, and general diffuſion of ſcience, learned men have deified human reaſon, and rejected the goſpel revelation; in lieu of which they have adopted ſyſtems the moſt contradictory and abſurd. The laſt menacing progreſs of infidelity has been accelerated, by the immoral lives of thoſe, who ought to have adorned the ſanctuary of God by their wiſdom and virtues. Jeſus Chriſt, the prophets and apoſtles, have been aſſociated with antichriſtian prieſts, and the whole ridiculed as a ſucceſſion of hypocrites and impoſtors.*—Here we adore the wiſdom of Providence, which obliges thoſe very men, who ſpeak ſo contumeliouſly or the ſacred writers, to confer upon them the higheſt honour, by accompliſhing their predictions in a manner ſo ſtriking and correct. O may the remaining part, the catholics who ſtill continue in idolatry, be " affrighted and give glory to God " by a ſcriptural reform, leſt they drink of the cup of his indignation.

We ſhall now proceed to illuſtrate ſome other prophecies, which are extremely full and explicit reſpecting the univerſal ſpread of the goſpel, previous to the total fall of antichriſt, and the deſtruction of unbelievers. " This goſpel of the kingdom," ſays Jeſus, " ſhall be preached in all the world for a witneſs unto all nations, and then ſhall the end come. Matt. xv. 14. The Son of Man—ſhall ſend his angels " or miniſters " with a great ſound of the trumpet, and they ſhall gather together his elect from the four winds, from one end of the heaven to the

---

* Voltaire on Toleration. Gibbon on the Decline and Fall of the Roman Empire.

other. v 31 —I faw an angel," fays John, " fly in the midft of heaven, having the everlafting gofpel to preach unto them that dwell on the earth, and to every nation and kindred, and tongue and people, faying with a loud voice, fear God, and give glory unto him, for the hour of his judgment is come. and worfhip him that made heaven and earth, and the fea, and the fountains of water And there followed another angel, faying, Babylon is fallen, is fallen, &c " Rev xiv 6, 7, 8, From thefe paffages and others of the fame import, we learn, that the gofpel fhall be preached in every ifland, nation, and language and preached amid the four winds or troubles that fhall afflict all nations, that the holy angels fhall have a fpecial charge to fuperintend the glorious work, that the miffions are fure to fucceed for the heathens fhall forfake their temples, and worfhip the God that made heaven and earth. that this fhall take place previous to the total fall of the fpiritual Babylon As its fall is predicted in four or five places in the revelation, it feems to be the order of Providence, that it fhould fall at fo many different periods.

To revive religion in the degenerate church and diffufe it univerfally abroad, will require an immenfe number of inftruments; and here the harmony of revelation and providence will be made confpicuous. The fpirit of life from God fhall enter into his faithful witneffes, and they fhall afcend to heaven that is, be promoted to places of eminence in the church and in prefence of their unbelieving enemies All hurtful diftinctions between the clergy and the laity, which have intimidated the latter from ufing their gifts of prayer and exhortation in religious affemblies, fhall be abolifhed. God will pour forth his fpirit upon his fervants and handmaidens in thofe days, and they fhall prophecy Joel ii So it was in the primitive church every man among them was enjoined to pray or preach according to the abilities which God had given him by the holy fpirit Rom xii Thus fhall the Lord of the harveft, fend forth plenty of labourers into his vineyard.

The converfion of the jews, it is prefumed will take place at an earlier period, during the fpread of the gofpel among the heathens. Exclufive of the years of their exile, which God can fhorten, if they humble themfelves before him, the fhameful lives of profeffed chriftians have been the greateft obftruction to their converfion. The Rabbins have juftly concluded, that they might as well remain as they be ftill, and lead fuch lives as moft chriftians do. But when the identical world fhall have renounced the chriftian faith, and seceded from religious assemblies, the church will exhibit her primitive graces, and conciliate the affections of her enemies, and the missionaries having considerably succeeded abroad, will have roiled away our reproach among the heathens, and rendered the christian name respectable in all the earth The accordance of these events, on the one hand, and the Jews being wearied and hopeless in their misguided expectations of the Messiah, on the other, will induce them to search the scriptures with fasting and prayer Then shall the veil which is upon their hearts, when Moses and the prophets are read, be taken away, and they will discover this grand point, that the Messiah was to be cut off, and his soul made an offering for sin, before he was to see his seed, prolong his days, and see the pleasure of the Lord prosper in his hands Isa liii.

The God of Abraham hath disposed of his ancient people for purposes subservient to his gracious providence He hath not cast them away, nor forgotten his covenant, to give them the land " for an everlasting possession " Jerusalem shall be trodden down of the Gentiles only, until the times of the Gentiles be fulfilled And even now, while he punishes their incredulity, he makes them a proof of the authenticity of those scriptures, which predicted their dispersion, and announce their return Deut xxviii 64 Isa xi 11 Among idolaters they communicate the knowledge of the true God , and among christians and deists, they demonstrate the sad consequences of making light of the gospel, and rejecting the Lord of life and glory But his judgments are blended with mercies Dwelling among all commercial nations, and being perfectly acquainted with their manners, customs, languages and religions, they are already arranged as an army of missionaries Their situation is peculiarly happy for the conversion of the Turks, Tartars, Persians, and the numerous nations on the African shores When that is the case, " Ethiopia shall soon stretch out her hands unto God " Psal lxviii 31 And surely an event, so important and long expected, would remove the languor and lukewarmness of the christian world. Of this we may be confident, that whenever they shall embrace the Messiah, whom their fathers crucified, and be endowed with the " residue of the spirit," Mal ii 15, their sermons will not be cold and indifferent, but warm and current, like those of St Paul, and the other apostles , and such as will fill the church with acclamations of joy and thanksgiving " If the casting away of Israel were the reconciling of the world, what shall the receiving of them be but life from the dead ? Rom. xi. 15.

While these desirable events are taking place in the church Satan and the deistical world will not remain inactive. But it is presumed that God will restrain the latter from any severe persecution of his saints. They will be busied in applying their modern philosophy to politics, laws, and literature, and scarce observe the progress of the gospel. These men are likely to shake all nations, and to destroy one another by a succession of wars and factions. Meanwhile, let the ministers, after the wise example of their master, keep clear of all political parties; and pray fervently for those princes and magistrates which afford them protection. Let them be wise as serpents, harmless as doves, and bold as lions, and if the calamities of war should visit their country, let them " enter the closet and hide for a small moment until the indignation be overpast. When ye shall hear of wars and rumours of wars, be not terrified, neither let your heart be afraid. the end is not yet.—In your patience possess ye your souls.—The hairs of your head are all numbered." Luke xx

It is apparent, from the sixteenth chapter of the Revelation, that during the decline of the Papal empire, God shall pour out the seven last vials of his wrath upon the wicked. Five of these, it is presumed by the ingenious Jurieu, have already been poured out; and the sixth, which is to fall upon the Euphrates or Mahometan empire, may open the way for the Jews to return. When that period is come, it is easy with God to raise up some Cyrus to bring them back. " If they abide not still in unbelief, God is able to graft them in again." As unbelief was the principal cause which occasioned their dispersion, in my opinion, it is highly improbable, they should be gathered in a state of infidelity and wickedness, and in such case, the advantages of their present happy situation, for preaching the gospel to all nations, would escape unimproved. These are the reasons which have induced me to deviate from the common opinion, and to believe, that there will be a great work of God among the Jews before they are gathered, or not more than a partial gathering before their conversion. When they see the heathen isles and nations begin to do homage to the Messiah, they will recognize the accomplishment of prophecy, and flame to be the first to embrace their King. " Blindness in part is happened to Israel until the fulness of the gentiles be come in. And so all Israel shall be saved in the day of the Lord." Rom xi 25, 26.

Being visited—in strange lands—with the grace and comforts of the gospel, they shall be emboldened to return to Salem, and to accomplish all those glorious things which are spoken of the city of God. They shall gather their treasures of gold and silver, and merchandise, and accompanied by artificers of every description, shall build the city and temple of the Lord, and shall worship him with sacrifices and peace-offerings, and thanksgivings, as described by Ezekiel the prophet, ch. xl to xlviii. Some shall go by land, and floods of difficulties shall flow back and give them passage. Others shall go by sea, "and the ships of Tarshish shall bring his sons" says God "from afar, and his daughters from the ends of the earth. They shall return and come to Zion with singing, and everlasting joy shall be upon their heads, they shall obtain joy and gladness, and sorrow and sighing shall flee away." Isa. xi. xxxv. 8. See also Isa. 11. 2, 4. xxxii. xlii, 8. xlv. 14, 15, 16. These predictions are totally inapplicable to the return of the Jews from the Babylonian captivity, They did not return by sea, nor did the sons of strangers build their walls. The people were not all righteous, their peace was not uninterrupted, and their city and temple were not an eternal excellency. All these events must in vain be accounted for, or the established rules of interpreting prophecy by Usher, Mede, More, and Newton, must be given up !!!

The destruction of idolatry, and the universal spread of the gospel, will indeed be highly gratifying to the saints, but at the same time, they are connected with such other visitations of Providence, as should induce us to "rejoice with trembling." For in that eventful day, God will most awfully punish the unbelieving world. There is scarce a text which speaks of the kingdom of Christ, in which his destroying the unbelieving is not expressed or implied. When he takes the heathen for his inheritance, and the uttermost parts of the earth for his possession, he will break the wicked as a potter's vessel, with a rod of iron. Psalm ii. "The nation that will not serve thee shall be destroyed, yea, it shall be utterly wasted away. Isa. lx. 12. In those days shall be affliction, such as was not since the beginning of the creation which God created, unto this time, neither shall be any more.—Take heed to yourselves, lest at any time your heart be overcharged with surfeiting and drunkenness, and with the cares of this life, and so that day come upon you unawares. For as a snare shall it come upon all them that dwell on the face of the w[hole ea]r[th]

PART I. Watch, therefore, and pray that ye may be able to escape all those things that shall come to pass, and to stand before the Son of Man." Luke xxi. O that the deist may hear this and tremble, and cast away his infidelity, lest God fight against him with the sword that goeth out of his mouth.

These events are distant and indistinct. At present we can have but an imperfect notion of them, nor will they be fully understood till the time of their completion. Let us, therefore, be content with improving the light we have. It seems, that the unbelieving part of the nations, who shall have hardened themselves against the gospel, will yet be more hardened under the judgments of God. The immense riches, extensive commerce, and incomparable prosperity of the Jews, will be the wonder of the age. Those riches will operate on the avarice of unbelieving princes, and the weak and defenceless state of the country, will embolden their passion for military fame.

This posture of affairs, will be deemed by Satan too favourable a moment to let slip, without making a last combined but ineffectual efforts to recover his ruined empire. "The lying spirit shall go forth out of the mouth of the dragon, and out of the mouth of the beast, and out of the mouth of the false prophet, to the kings of the earth, and of the whole world, to gather them to the battle of that great day of God Almighty. Rev. xvi. 13, 14. The ostensible plea for this war may be, (for the lying spirits will affect to speak the truth,) that the concourse of strangers who resort to Judea, and the very flourishing state of the Jewish commerce, are injurious to the interests, and subversive to the commerce of all other nations; These hardened princes of the earth, who have refused to obey the gospel, shall combine and surround the Holy Land with immense armies of their ungodly subjects, and greatly alarm and terrify the Jews. "In that day there shall be a great mourning in Jerusalem, as the mourning of Hadad-rimmon in the valley of Megiddon, and the land shall mourn, every family apart —And they shall look on him whom they have pierced." Zech. xii. All their expectations of deliverance shall be in the arm of the crucified Messiah, who shall regard their affliction, and speedily come to save them. "In that day shall the Lord defend the inhabitants of Jerusalem, and he that is feeble among them shall be as David. Behold I will make Jerusalem a cup of trembling unto all the people round about, when

B

they shall be in the siege both against Judea and against Jerusalem. —All that burden themselves with it shall be cut to pieces, though all the people of the earth were gathered against it. Zech. xii 2, 8   The hand of the Lord shall be known towards his servants, and his indignation towards his enemies " Isa lxii. 14   Ezekiel, in his views of this awful destruction of the infidel world, seems to have been more favoured than any of the antient prophets   In the thirty-eighth and thirty-ninth chapters, we are informed at large, that the allied hosts of Gog and Magog shall assemble from Persia, Ethiopia, and the countries which surround Judea; that taking advantage of the unfortified state of the country, they shall combine to ravage it, that the Lord shall destroy them with hail and flames of fire, leaving but a sixth part to escape, and that the bury of their dead bodies shall continue seven months.

But the most sublime description of Christ's coming to destroy those who will not have him to reign over them, is found in the nineteenth chapter of the Revelation   I saw heaven opened," says John. ' and behold a white horse, and he that sat upon him was called faithful and true, and in righteousness he doth judge and make war   And his eyes were as a flame of fire, and on his head were many crowns, and he had a name written that no man knew but he himself. and he was clothed with a vesture dipped in blood, and his name is called the word of God   And the armies which were in heaven followed him upon white horses, clothed in fine linen, white and clean   And out of his mouth goeth a sharp sword, that with it he should smite the nations; and he shall rule them with a rod of iron   and he shall tread the wine press of the fierceness and wrath of Almighty God.   And he hath on his vesture, and on his thigh a name written, KING of kings, and LORD of lords —And I saw an angel standing in the sun, and he cried with a loud voice, saying to all the fowls that fly in the midst of heaven, come, gather yourselves together unto the supper of the great God, that ye may eat the flesh of kings, and the flesh of captains, and the flesh of mighty men, and the flesh of horses, and the flesh of them that sit on them, and the flesh of all men both bond and free, both small and great —And I saw the BEAST, and the kings of the earth, gathered together to make war against him that sat on the horse, and against his army   And the beast was taken, and with him the false prophet that wrought miracles before him, with which he deceived them that had the mark of the beast, and them that worshiped his image These both were cast alive into a lake of fire burning with brimstone And the remnant were slain with the sword of him that sat on the horse.—And all the fowls were filled with their flesh "

We have now observed, the progress of the gospel among the isles and nations of the heathens, that it shall bid defiance to the powers of Antichrist, the sneers of infidelity, and the wide influence of hoary idolatry. The Lord God will be with his servants and ensure their success. " Every valley shall be exalted, every mountain and hill shall be made low, and the crooked shall be made straight, and the rough places plain and the glory of the Lord shall be revealed, and—all flesh—shall see it—together; for the mouth of the Lord hath spoken it All the ends of the world shall remember and turn unto the Lord, and all kindred of the nations shall worship before thee " Isa xl 4, 5 Psal xxii 27. It now remains that we take a view of the scripture doctrine respecting

THE GLORIOUS MILLLNIUM.

I The happy age before us, which has so long been the cheering theme of prophecy, and the support of the church in all her struggles with the pagan and the papal beast, shall be ushered in by a personal, though transient manifestation of the Son of God In addition to what is said above, there are other scriptures, not less clear and explicit in confirmation of this doctrine " Behold " says John, " he cometh with clouds, and every eye shall see him, they also which have pierced him shall wail because of him " Rev i 7. This passage has an evident allusion to the twelfth chapter of Zechariah " And they shall look on him whom they have pierced " Hence it is the more proper to apply it to the manifestation of the Son of God at this eventful period " Whom the heavens " says Peter, " must receive until the times of the—restitution—of all things, which God hath spoken by the mouth of his holy prophets since the world began Acts i 21 Then will the Lord go forth and fight against those [infidel] nations, as when he fought [for Joshua] in the day of battle And his feet shall stand in that day on the mount of Olives, which is before Jerusalem on the east, and the mount of Olives shall cleave in the midst thereof towards the east, and towards the west and there shall be a great valley, and half of the mountain shall remove toward the north, and half of it toward the south —And the Lord my God shall come, and all the saints with thee And it shall come to pass in that day, that the light shall not be clear nor dark But it shall be one day which shall be known to the Lord, not day nor night, but it shall come to pass at evening time it shall be light." Zech xiv 4, 8

II The glorious manifestation of the Son of God, shall at the same instant, be accompanied with ten thousand prodigies and happy events both in the kingdom of nature and of grace. The bodies of all the holy martyrs, who during the pagan and the antichristian persecutions were beheaded for the witness of Jesus, and for the word of God shall be raised up from the dead. Their useful lives were shortened on earth, and therefore God shall honour them with an earlier resurrection; and, it seems, with an angelic ministry in his kingdom and they shall live and reign with Christ a thousand years. This is the first resurrection. "Blessed and holy is he that hath part in the first resurrection on such the second death hath no power, but they shall be priests of God, and of Christ, and shall reign with him a thousand years" Rev xx 4, 5, 6 Where this reign of Christ and the holy martyrs shall be, we are not permitted to know it is said only, " I saw thrones, and they sat upon them " It is indeed said, by the twenty-four elders, " Thou hast made us unto our God kings and priests; and we shall reign [over] the earth " Rev v 10 But I think it has no peculiar reference to the millenium it rather refers to the promise made to the apostles Matt, xix 28, and Luke xxii. 29, 30. As our Lord hath said, that the children of the resurrection are equal unto the angels; and as St Paul has distinguished their offices by the dignified appellatives of—thrones—dominions—principalities—and powers, it is not improbable but the holy martyrs will be raised to an angelic ministry in the kingdom of heaven, and to superintend the church in all that glorious prosperity, which they so often prayed for and desired to see while on earth The Lord " will create upon every dwelling place of Mount Zion, and upon his assemblies, a cloud and a smoke by day, and the shining of a flaming fire by night for upon all the glory shall be a defence ' If iv 5 Should this application of these prophecies be admitted as just, it by no means follows, that those who sit on the thrones, and the reigning martyrs will visibly converse with mortals, therefore, all the objections which have been made against their reigning with Christ on earth, fall to the ground

III To the victory of our Lord over the infidel world, shall immediately succeed the binding and imprisonment of satan in the bottomless pit for a thousand years " After that he must be loosed for a little season " Rev xx 3 O how glorious will be the state of the church, and flourishing the work of grace upon the soul, when the hosts of demons are chased away from this lower region, and their places supplied with the holy martyrs, when we shall have every spiritual aid, and no spiritual obstruction!!!

IV The manifestation of the Lord is also represented as attended with " a great and mighty earthquake " Zech xiv 5. This with other changes which will then take place in the kingdom of nature, may produce the most benignant effects on the elements, and on the fertility of the earth There shall be springs in the deserts and pools in the parched ground Isa xxxv. The vagrant sands of Arabia shall be imprisoned ; the country covered with vegetation, and its vallies replenished with rivers The bituminous waters of the lake of Sodom, shall be healed by a river from the house of God, and fishermen shall spread their nets on its banks Ezek xlvii 1, 12 Of this we have a moral certainty, that the barrenness of the earth, and the obstructions of husbandry were designed to punish and restrain the wickedness of the nations, and when that wickedness shall be diminished, the righteous God will also proportionably diminish the difficulties of agriculture The holy scriptures put this beyond a doubt, and assure us, that the produce of the earth shall then exceed all possible calculation. So luxuriant shall be the harvest, that it shall continue till the vintage, and the vintage shall continue till the seed time " The mountains shall drop down new wine, and the hills shall flow with milk, and the rivers of Judah shall flow with waters, and a fountain shall come of the house of the Lord, and shall water the valley of Shittim Joel iii 18 Then shall the earth yield its increase, and God, even our own God, shall bless us Psal lxvii. 6.

V. The increase of population shall correspond with the abundance of vegetation, and with the agriculture and industry of the husbandman " A little one shall become a thousand, and a strong one a great nation —Behold the days come saith the Lord, that the city shall be built to the Lord, from the tower of Hananeel unto the gate of the corner , and the measuring line shall yet go forth over against it upon the hill Gareb, and shall compass about to Goath. And the whole valley of the dead bodies, and of the ashes, and all the fields unto the brook Kidron, unto the corner of the horse gate toward the east, shall be holy unto the Lord, it shall not be plucked up or thrown down, any more for ever " Jer xxxi. 38, 40 All the waste and desolate places shall be inhabited, the increase of population shall be such as to require emigrations, for the land shall be too narrow The children of succeeding generations shall say to their fathers, " The place is too strait for me, —give place that I may dwell " Isa xlix 20 So numerous and great are the blessings, which shall descend on this lower world, at the times of the restitution of all things, as may in a qualified sense, be termed—a new creation " Behold I create new heavens and a new earth —I create Jerusalem a rejoicing, and her people a joy And I will rejoice in Jerusalem, and joy in my people; and the voice of weeping shall no more be heard in her, nor the voice of crying There shall no more be thence an infant of days, nor an old man that hath not filled his days, for the child shall die an hundred years old, but the sinner being an hundred years old shall be accursed —And they shall build houses, and inhabit them, and they shall plant vineyards, and eat of the fruit of them. They shall not build, and another inhabit; they shall not plant, and another eat, for, as the days of a tree, are the days of my people, and mine elect shall long enjoy the work of their hands.—The inhabitants shall not say —I am sick ; for the people shall be forgiven their iniquities " Isa lxv 17, &c From this view of the latter day's glory, we learn, that mankind will be then much exempt from disease, and die in a very old age, that there will be few wicked men, and that this new earth must be different from that mentioned by Peter and John, because death will be here, and some instances of wickedness

VI In that happy age, the peace of society and the intercourse of commerce, will not be interrupted by the sound of the trumpet or the roaring of cannon, for God shall make wars to cease to the end of the earth. Psal xlvi 9 " Nation shall not lift up sword against nation, neither shall they learn war any more." In that populous state of the world, the wild beasts, of course, will be few, and all domesticated ' The wolf shall lie down with the lamb, and the leopard shall lie down with the kid, and the calf, and the young lion, and the fatling together, and the little child shall lead them And the cow and the bear shall feed, and their young ones shall lie down together, and the lion .

shall eat straw like the ox —They shall not hurt nor destroy in all my holy mountain " Isa. xi. 5, 6, 7, 9.

VII Great and inestimable are the blessings already enumerated, but they are very inconsiderable, if compared with the graces and talents which God shall communicate to the saints, and with the unction of the Spirit which shall rest on all religious assemblies The pentecost will then extend to all the earth, and every nation exhibit primitive Christianity arrived to vigorous maturity The superabundance of knowledge, graces, and gifts, will in some sort, constitute the whole church, a royal priesthood unto God They shall all be righteous and they shall no more teach every man his neighbour, and every man his brother, saying,—know the Lord for they shall all know him from the least to the greatest —The earth shall be full of the knowledge of the Lord as waters cover the sea

The public worship of that age will have a striking resemblance of heaven, and immense congregations be overshadowed with the Divine presence All hardness and obduracy shall be removed from the mind, all iniquity forgiven, and the laws of Christ written on every heart. When they pray, the Lord will answer, and when they call, he will say —here am I The people shall shout and sing the praises of their God, and the Lord shall rain down righteousness upon them His glory shall enter his holy temple in justice, by the east-gate, and dwell on the mercy-seat. He will make the place of his feet glorious in the midst of them, and he will beautify the house of his glory His altars shall no more be attended, nor his sanctuary filled, with priests and ministers that dishonour his name, but he will give the people pastors after his own heart, who shall feed them with knowledge and understanding Isa xl Ezek xliii Jer iii 15

Kings, princes, and the most illustrious characters, shall esteem it their highest honour to be the messengers of the churches, to bring gifts and offerings to the house of God, and to worship before him Nor shall one nation be jealous of another, " for the Lord shall be king in all the earth His dominion shall be from sea to sea, and from the river to the ends of the earth —The kingdom, and dominion, and greatness of the kingdom under the whole heaven, shall be given unto the people of the Most High, whose kingdom is an everlasting kingdom, and all dominions shall serve and obey him —The zeal of the Lord of hosts will perform this.' Psal lxxii Dan. vii. Isa ix. 6.

Rife crown'd with grace, imperial Salem rife !
Exalt thy tow'ry head, and lift thine eyes,
See, a long race thy fp..ious courts adorn,
See future fons and daughters yet unborn !
See barb'rous nations at thy gates attend,
Walk in thy light, and in thy temple bend ,
See thy bright altars throng'd with proftrate kings,
And heap'd with products of Sabæan fprings !
For thee Idume's fpicy torefts blow,
And feeds of gold in Ophir's mountains glow.
See heav'n its fparkling portals wide d fplay,
And break upon thee in a flood of day
. .   .   .   .   .   The light himfelf fhall fhine
Reveal'd, and God's eternal day be thine.   POPE

"Mafter," faid the difciples, "when fhall thefe things be,
—and what figns will there be when thefe things fhall come to
pafs" Our Lord faid nothing of the time ; but he condefcend-
ed to give them the figns and tokens of his approach, which
indicates, that the prophecies refpecting the laft times will be
underftood by the wife, whenever thefe figns fhall appear.
John in many of his vifions, faw the temple of God fill'ed with
fmoke, importing that the ways of the Moft High are profound and impenetrable , but when providence fhall have com-
mented on prophecy, his ways fhall be made manifeft, and
heaven and earth fhall give glory to his name for the riches of
his mercy and the equity of his juftice.

In diftinguifhing the difpenfations of God, the facred writers
moftly exprefs themfelves in the plural number "The times
and feafons —The times of the reftitution of all things —The
ages paft —The laft times —And the laft day. And, as the
paft difpenfations have exceeded one another in manifeftations
of truth and grace, on the fame fcale, we are confident he will
more ftrikingly difplay, "in the ages to come, the exceeding riches
of his grace in his kindnefs towards us through Chrift Jefus."

That the latter day's glory of the church is now approach-
ing ; and that the prefent revivals of religion at home, and
miffions abroad, are preparatory to it, we have weighty reafons
for believing from the obvious calculation of prophecy. Daniel's
prophecy of the feventy weeks, counting a prophetic day for a
year, for the Meffiah to be cut off, was accomplifhed at the
predicted period. According to the fame calculation, the two
thoufand and three hundred days or years for the cleanfing the
fanctuary of its antichriftian corruptions, are thought by fome,

to be accomplished about this time Also, the time, times, and half time —The three days and a half day —The forty two months —The twelve hundred and sixty days or years, which are similar periods for the man of sin to preside in the temple of God, are thought to be nearly expired. But it is said, by Daniel, that the abomination which maketh defolate, should continue in the holy place, a thousand two hundred and ninety days, and then adds; " blessed is he that waiteth, and cometh to the thousand three hundred and five and thirty days." xii, 11, 12.   The first of these numbers, feems to allow a period of thirty days or years for the cleansing of the holy place of its corruptions ; and the second, a period of feventy five days or years for the propagation of the gospel and introduction of the happy age

What a glorious and defirable state of things is here before us"! A world—full of people, and full of plenty   No demons in the air, to inflame the passions, foment infiduous factions, and kindle war among the nations   Virtue and truth, reigning in fociety ; and health, peace, and joy, blooming on every countenance — But they must have their day of probation   God hath largely diversified his dispensations towards mankind, but hath never interrupted our moral liberty, or accepted any fervices of man that were not voluntary   Accordingly, at the expiration of the thoufand years, Satan shall be loofed out of prifon, and shall go out to deceive the nations, &c Rev. xx 7 to 10

An awful obfcurity veils thefe events, which are fo diftant and indiftinct ; and at prefent it feems too daring to comment on the loofing of Satan, further than that the piety of this happy age, shall hereby be put to the teft   However it is conjectured, that he will not prefume, at firft, to feduce them into grofs wickedness But finding them dwelling under a benignant fky, and on a foil that might vie with Paradife, he will endeavour to enfnare them, by the luxuries of their table, which muft fpeedily produce effeminacy, idlenefs, and want   and want may induce them to extort fupplies from thofe who have plenty. From depredation and plunder, they may eafily meafure back their fteps into the follies and vices of the apoftate ages   At leaft, it is apprehended, this may be the cafe, with great numbers, in different parts of the earth. This conjecture feems the more probable, becaufe this happy age will not be wholly free from wickedness and by confequence, not only free from lukewarmness in religion. How needful, even then, for every one to watch, and to fee that his foul be truly alive to God, left he fall in the day of trial. Thefe apoftates having caufed fevere afflictions to the church in many places, may at length be hardened to rebel aguinft the Lord, and againft the beloved city, which will be ftored with riches and plenty, and be led on by the devil to their own deftruction, as the firft army of Gog and Magog were led on by the lying fpirits

Whether this notion of the apoftacy be proper or improper, or whatever fuceefs Satan may have among the nations, we are affured by many promifes, that he will have little fuccefs againft the church in Judea. " As I have fworn that the waters of Noah fhould no more go over the earth , fo have I fworn that I will not be wroth with thee, nor rebuke thee For the mountains fhall depart, and the hills be removed; but my kindnefs fhall not depart from thee, neither fhall the covenant of my peace be removed, faith the Lord, that hath mercy on thee —Thy fun fhall no more go down, neither fhall thy moon wane ; for the Lord fhall be thine everlafting light, and the days of thy mourning fhall be ended." Ifa liv 9, 10, lx 20.

Short indeed will be this laft ftruggle of the common enemy ; for the Lord Jefus fhall be revealed from heaven in flaming fire, to furprife and punifh the apoftate multitudes " As it was in the days of Noah, fo fhall the coming of the Son of Man be. They were eating and drinking, marrying and giving in marriage, and the flood came and deftroyed them all Luke xvii 27. ' I faw " fays John, " a great white throne, and him that fat on it, from whofe face the earth and the heaven fled away, and there was found no place for them And I faw the dead, fmall and great, ftand before God ; and the books were opened and another book was opened, which is the book of life and the dead were judged out of thofe things which were written in the books, according to their works And death and hell were caft into the lake of fire. This is the fecond death. And whofoever was not found written in the book of life, was caft into the lake of fire." Rev xx 11, 15

What a train of folemnities is here ! The diffolution of heaven and earth A world of fpirits receiving their bodies a fecond time from the duft and as the fhepherds ufed to clear the forefts, and feparate the fheep from the goats, fo are the wicked forever feparated from the good. How glorious and how qualified is the judge!!! He searched all hearts, and there is no secret but is manifest to the eyes of him with whom we have *to do*! The books are opened and correspond with the copy in every man's bosom: as a person walking over soft ground leaves the print of his steps behind, so are all the motions of our hearts recorded here. Every man is judged according to his works,—his talents,—and his dispensation. The heathen is judged according to the law of nature; the Jew according to the law of Moses, and the christian according to the gospel. In righteousness God shall judge the world.

And oh! how will the wicked bear to see him, whom they have rejected and blasphemed, now exalted to ineffable glory and dominion? His members whom they have persecuted and contemned, now seated on thrones? How will they bear to see the incomparable love of Christ, now turned into high disdain, his long suffering and meekness changed into fury and revenge; to hear that voice which so often pronounced blessings, and find —come, now say, depart ye cursed into everlasting fire, prepared for the devil and his angels.—They have despised his mercy, and must revere his justice, they have hated the light, and darkness is their dwelling, they have rejected eternal happiness, and everlasting misery is their portion. What—separated from God—from all good—and hope forever lost!!! Oh! how insupportable the thought! Let the sinner timely hearken to Moses and the prophets, to Christ and the apostles, that he come not into that place of torment.

The scene shall close by the accession of the righteous to the new and everlasting kingdom of our Lord and Saviour Jesus Christ. Their bodies shall be inconceivably beautiful, perfect, and luminous, like the glorified humanity of Christ. Their capacity of happiness shall be matured and enlarged: the many powers and affections of the soul which are now obscured in ignorance and infirmity shall then be unfolded, and gratified with consumate happiness. It shall be ennobled with a proper degree of intuitive knowledge, immutably fixed in the love of God, and no more assailed with the temptation, or afflicted with evil. Consequently the mediatorial kingdom shall cease, and be delivered up to God, even the Father. Then shall we see,—and O that God may count us worthy to see,—the Lord Jesus, who is above every name that is named, at the head of his church, which is his body, and the fulness of him that filleth all in all. Rivers of knowledge, and pleafure, and happinefs, and life, fhall flow from his throne, and deluge the kingdom with the fulnefs of eternal joy. In the adminiftration of his eternal providence, he fhall continue to difclofe the amazing wonders of his love, which fhall charm the happy worlds before the throne, and infpire them with boundlefs variety of happinefs, ever new and increafing in delight. But here, like infant princes, who are unacquainted with the dignity of their birth, we are unable to anticipate the felicity of that better world. It hath not entered the heart of man, the things that God hath prepared for them that love him. May the Almighty affift us to apprehend them more ftrongly by faith, and by a larger enjoyment of them in our hearts, that we may rejoice in hope, and trample on the vanities of this world, for the glory that fadeth not away.

To conclude, in this view of the univerfal fpread of chriftianity, and glorious millenium, I have followed the fteps of others warily, and have differed from them, as the proximity of thefe events may have reflected clearer light upon the fubjects. The ancient fathers, did not underftand the nature of the antichriftian empire; but we find Papias, Juftin Martyr, Iræneus, Nepos, Victorinus, Lactantius, and Sulpicius Severus, among thofe who warmly efpoufed the doctrine of the millenium. Within this and the laft century, Archbifhop Ufher, Bifhop Newton, Dr. Owen, Dr. Gill, Mr Fletcher, Mr. W and a moft refpectable train of other divines both at home and abroad, have written upon the fubject and to thefe writings I am much indebted for the imperfect notions which I have of this happy period.

But while we afk, when the kingdom of God fhall come: let us not like the fcribes and pharifees, neglect to look for it in our own hearts. If it be not there, in vain fhould we be permitted to fee it in the church. Except a man be converted, and become as a little child, he fhall in no-wife enter the kingdom of heaven.

FINIS.

CPSIA information can be obtained
at www.ICGtesting.com
Printed in the USA
BVHW020751090223
658123BV00040B/480